Purposeful Cultures

A PRACTICAL SELF-LEADERSHIP GUIDE

satisfaction
collaboration
self-awareness
systemic awareness
productivity resilience
adaptability
meaningful work
engagement wellbeing
culture
creativity
joy confidence
mindset

Dr Josie McLean

Published by The Partnership Pty Ltd

Cover design by James McLean © The Partnership Pty Ltd

Third edition 2024

ISBN: 978 0 6488650 2 5

The Partnership Pty Ltd
PO Box 192
Blackwood, South Australia 5051 Australia
drjosiemclean.com

DEDICATION

*I dedicate this workbook to all those people
who have been taught
that they must endure work.*

*My hope is that you will be liberated
to find purposeful, nurturing work.*

*Work that serves you, your organisation,
your customers,
and community, and the
more-than-human world.*

CONTENTS

CARING

Don't impose on me what you know,

I want to explore the unknown

And be the source of my own discoveries.

Let the known be my liberation, not my slavery.

The world of your truth can be my limitation.

Your wisdom my negation.

Don't instruct me; let's walk together.

Let my richness begin where yours ends.

Show me so that I can stand

On your shoulders.

Reveal yourself so that I can be

Something different.

You believe that every human being

Can love and create.

I understand, then, your fear

When I ask you to live according to your wisdom.

You will not know who I am

By listening to yourself.

Don't instruct me; let me be.

Your failure is that I be identical to you.

By Marcial Losada

Inspired by Umberto Maturana's "The Student's Prayer"

FOREWORD

As I read through this book, I reflected on significant and positive impact Josie's work had on us at the City of Marion. Josie brought our Senior Management (the 3 senior levels) together with a common purpose and unlocked the contribution and leadership of everyone, particularly engaging 3rd level. It was both liberating and energising. Amazing! Her work also focussed on our emerging leaders. Developing our constructive leaders for the future from within was our vision. Josie led our "Emerging Leaders Program" a 12 month program which we ran annually to prepare our future leaders to be successful stewards of change. I saw so many people find their voice with a purity of purpose. Altruistic! Their contributions increased immediately, and we knew we now had our future leaders.

Josie's contribution is recognised as a very important contribution to the transformation of the organisational culture and performance of Marion. In 2000 the City of Marion embarked on a suite of strategies to address long term persistent operating deficits (12% plus), high staff turnover (above 20%), customer service, major project failure, and a broad range of persistent operational issues. The foundation for these strategies was a solid commitment to using Human Synergistics methodology to transform the organisational culture and develop a highly constructive organisation supported by highly constructive leadership. By 2006 Marion was recognised for being one of the top 3 financially managed councils in South Australia. Marion was also recognised with 4 Cultural Transformation Awards (2007, 09, 11 & 13) and the City remains a case study on the Human Synergistics' website. Marion also received bronze and Gold Australian Business Excellence Awards (2007 & 2010) alongside many private sector companies.

In reading this book I recognised aspects of the leadership development experience Josie provided us. I could also see how she has continued to refine and develop her approach to be increasingly more constructively impactful. It is a fantastic resource, and it is my absolute pleasure to recommend it to you.

Mark Searle
CEO, City of Marion
2000 to 2015

ENDORSEMENTS

"In *Purposeful Cultures,* Josie shares some key insights on leadership with reference to systems thinking. The world looks very different when you see yourself as part of a greater whole. Josie re-frames leadership accordingly, encouraging us to look beyond the idea of the leader as a wholly autonomous, rational being and to understand models of shared leadership. If we are part of a greater whole, then we need to be good at listening and seeking to understand each other's perspectives. We need to explore how others think (their 'mental models') and to appreciate how those ways of thinking are similar/different to our own. This requires us to be self-aware and to appreciate more deeply how our ways of thinking have emerged and continue to evolve through our interaction with others. Josie picks up on all these themes in a short, easy to read, book full of reflective exercises."

- Dr Paul Lawrence, Principal at Leading Systemically

"Had I not attended the program accompanying this book, I may have ended up a very frustrated and angry person to work with. I didn't quite realise it then but it is so clear to me now, that you had quite literally given me the keys to my kingdom to be able to do meaningful and joyful work.

All I had to do was to believe you, that I had the capacity and appetite for small positive changes day-to-day to my mindset and habits.

It started with me trying to bring the best version of me to work. Somewhere along the way, it just became me really loving what I do and the people I work with."

- Calvin Puah, past participant of accompanying program

ABOUT THIS THIRD EDITION

The first edition of this book, written in 2012, was called The Equation. It was written as a workbook to accompany a self-leadership program of the same name that built upon the success of a leadership development program for middle managers. This success revealed a systemic weakness in organisational life; managers can change their ways of working, but their team members also need to explore different ways of thinking and being for optimal results. I started to notice that there were personal, structural, and cultural barriers to consider. Both the book and the programs explored what leadership and management might look like when we recognise and act upon our interdependence with everything – with other humans and the more-than-human world upon which we depend for life. That is, if we apply a systemic consciousness to our work within organisations and communities.

Ten years later, this third edition is now entitled *Purposeful Cultures,* and the update borrows heavily from the original book and adds what has been learned about systemic change in the course of a decade of delivery.

The name change also reflects the changing context in which we live and work. We are now post-pandemic and currently learning to live with COVID-19 in its endemic phase. Additionally, it is more apparent that humanity is at a crossroads and faces many systemic challenges, including:

- the ecological and climate emergency

- the unknown future of artificial intelligence as it intersects with the defence of countries

- an increasingly populated world

- a trend towards a more authoritarian, repressive political world.

How will we rise to these challenges? Will humanity survive? As you read the list of challenges above, I wonder if you immediately think these are overwhelming and not your concern. Be assured that how you choose to work and live contributes fundamentally to resolving these issues. All our 'smaller contributions' combine and accumulate over space and time into new patterns that either change the future or reinforce patterns that maintain the status quo. You and your choices matter.

Your leadership is required

Everything I have learned tells me that we must look to ourselves as 'the ones who will save us' – just as the well-known prophecy from the Hopi elders in 2000 encouraged us, "we are the ones we have been waiting for." It is time to redefine leadership from a position of authority to a role we all may choose. And it is time to learn to undertake this activity together – creating swirls of energy or movements to learn our way forward in these uncertain and exciting times, to make the differences that are being called for now.

I am working with you and your organisation to recognise the need for:

- each individual to be creative and adaptive and to contribute to the resilience of the organisation as it unfolds.

- you to be connected to each other and truly collaborate across silos, functions, disciplines and even sectors.

- sharing different perspectives if we are to understand the current reality our organisations face in an interconnected world.

Intended outcomes for you

Those at the leading edges of organisational and leadership development are adopting a systemic perspective that appreciates the whole system's Personal, Structural and Cultural facets (Figure 1). That means recognising whole people within whole systems and acting upon that perception. This book intends to focus attention on

Cultural

Structural

Personal

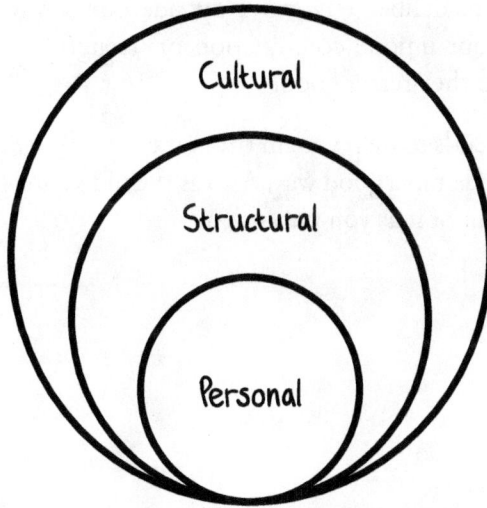

Figure 1: , The three facets of a systemic perspectiven

you and your personal leadership development within this broader context – recognising that no one can lead alone.

I bring a systemic perspective combined with insights from positive psychology to help you offer your best contribution during a time which is showing signs of being disruptive, challenging, and exciting in equal measures. Accepting this challenge to contribute all you can is good for your personal wellbeing and resilience, and I aim to support you in nurturing those qualities.

We all have an opportunity to engage purposefully with the systemic challenges much bigger than ourselves – which is a deeply satisfying way to live and work.

This requires each of us to help ourselves and each other to develop increased:

- self-awareness and self-management so that we are less reactive and more responsive in the company of others.

- collaborative capability to truly liberate our collective imagination and creativity in the form of experiments in new ways of living and working.

- courage to deliberately move outside our comfort zones and liberate our unique combination of strengths and insights in service to the greater good.

This book intends to help you, in the company of your colleagues, to challenge yourself in a good way. And as the old saying goes, you will get as much out of it as you put into it.

CHAPTER 1

Life and work on autopilot?

Questions addressed in this chapter:

- **Does life sometimes feel like you are stuck in the same day, over and over?**

- **How can you nurture a life by design?**

- **What topics does this book contain, and how do they relate to each other?**

How is your life? Is it as you imagined when you were little? Did you dream of being a doctor, or an astronaut, a teacher, a chef, an artist? What did you care deeply about? How is that care or concern expressed in your life and work today?

Some people, despite dreams of wonder when they were a child, feel that as an adult, they must face 'reality' and settle for much less - a life that is happy and comfortable on one level but unsatisfying on a deeper level. In coaching session after coaching session, conversations about career successes are accompanied by feelings of emptiness. There is a yearning for more – but for what?

Do you ever ask yourself, "Is that all there is?"

15

For many, life is reduced to a series of mundane cycles: wake up, go to work, do the same old stuff, come home, settle the kids, go to bed, and wake up ... It's like life on automatic pilot. People are living what the great naturalist-philosopher, Thoreau, called a life "of quiet desperation."

You don't have to settle for life on automatic pilot; indeed, I believe this is not the life intended for you... I believe there are many reasons why you may not be living more of the life you really want. But one major reason for many people is that they just haven't made the time to think about it much. And our lives are so busy that we aren't *encouraged* to think about it much either!

So, this book aims to help you 'to become everything one is capable of becoming' (Abraham Maslow) and live this life to its fullest! Maybe your life could be sweeter, more enjoyable, more fulfilling, more adventurous, and more rewarding. The path is not always easy, because we live in a world full of different systems (the major one being economic) that keep us living life on autopilot. This book will reveal how you might walk a path that reflects more conscious decisions about how you *really* want to live and work.

For instance, since the Enlightenment, or the 'Age of Reason', that began in the late 17th century, we in our modern western societies have been deeply socialised with unconscious assumptions about how the physical world works – like a physical clock – and how an advanced stage of society organises itself - using only hierarchy and authority. But biologists and ecologists in our own time are revealing that there are different types of systems – living systems – that behave nothing like clocks. And anthropologists and archaeologists are revealing that, in the past, humanity has organised itself in very different ways. Many societies were wary of authority and consciously developed social norms to ensure power was not exercised over people's free choice for extended periods of time. As we engage with the systemic challenges mentioned in the introduction, we may begin to recognise that we need to be more imaginative in organising our lives and work into the future. That all starts to sound a bit radical, but maybe, what we face is a crisis of *collective* imagination, creativity, and courage to try something different to what we are used to.

How can you nurture a life by design?

The key is to become aware of the largely unconscious choices you are already making and decide whether these choices still suit you – or not. The opportunity is to become more aware of who you truly are, what you have to offer and how you can contribute your best to, and with your family, friends, and workmates – and maybe future generations too.

The topics included in our journey of expanding awareness

To help you on your journey of self-discovery, awareness, and skill-building to contribute your best, I explore these topics:

- Becoming aware of our individual and collective unconscious assumptions.

- Raising your awareness of your unique combination of strengths, values, and sense of purpose.

- Becoming more conscious of yourself as a leader and understanding why your 'adaptive' leadership is required.

- Extending your skills of collaboration and influencing.

- Developing your awareness of how you can connect to and contribute best to your team and organisation.

The following model provides a map of our journey and how each part connects to and is interdependent with every other part.

Using this book

This book may be a companion to conversations you share either in a program delivered by my team or in the Discovery Circles program with your senior managers. Or you may be reading the book on your own, and if that is the case, I encourage you to discuss your reading with a friend, colleague, or family member. Conversations are vital because they support our ability to be conscious of our thinking and even to change our thinking. The book will serve as a record of the topics and discussions you will enjoy together – along with your emerging thoughts and insights.

Figure 2: Holonic map showing our focus of attention.

So, whether you are reading the book on your own or as part of a group, I encourage you to ponder the questions at the end of each chapter, undertake the fieldwork, and record your observations. Co-author the book with me and keep it as a record of your unique journey.

Your first reflection and self-assessment

1. On the next page, rate your life today on a scale from 1 to 10, indicating:

    a. Your awareness of cares or concerns that were important to you as a child or young adult – are you settling for something less than you really wanted?

    b. The degree of excitement or sense of adventure in your life/work.

    c. The time you spend on activities that give you deep satisfaction or joy in your life/work.

    d. Your ability to manage your own emotions and emotional reactions to circumstances.

e. Your courage to say what you genuinely think in ways that others can hear.

f. Your capability to lead or contribute to conversations that extend a group's current range of thinking.

g. Your sense of connection to your organisation's purpose and values.

	1	2	3	4	5	6	7	8	9	10
a.										
b.										
c.										
d.										
e.										
f.										
g.										

Consider what these ratings are telling you.

From what you have read so far, what are you feeling inspired by or curious to learn more about?

_____

_____

_____

_____

_____

_____

_____

CHAPTER 2

A fable and noticing mental models

Questions addressed in this chapter:

- **What are the dynamics of exercising leadership and facilitating change?**

- **What does it take to collaborate and nurture the 'greater good' for the whole?**

- **How does the way our brain functions influence the way we each perceive the world differently?**

A fable

This fable is adapted from David Hutchens' *Shadows of the Neanderthal,* which is an adaptation of Plato's "Allegory of the Cave". It features two characters:

Boogie: he, him

Farah: she, her

Once upon a time, five people lived together in a cave. In fact, these cave people had never left the cave. They sat inside every day of their lives, waiting for dead bugs and dry leaves to blow through the entrance so they could eat.

Each of the cave's occupants had different ideas about what was beyond the mouth of the cave, whether it was a dragon waiting to eat them, a giant god hell-bent on squishing them, or just a vast expanse of nothingness. They were so sure that nothing good was outside that they never even faced the cave entrance; they spent their whole lives looking at the cave walls, watching shadows of passing animals.

21

These cave people knew nothing of the true form of the animals, just the suggestions hinted at by shadows. Shadows, dead bugs, and sunburnt backs were all that the world had to offer. This was their truth, and they were satisfied with it. At least they could live lives full of certainty about what tomorrow would bring, and in this way, they were comfortable.

Until one morning, as he chewed thoughtfully on the tail of a dried-out centipede, one of the cave folk, Boogie, wondered aloud what might be beyond the mouth of the cave.

After several seconds of uncomfortable silence, Boogie's cave-brethren let loose with a unanimously negative reaction. Boogie's tribe shouted at him about the dangers of the outside world; they jeered, called him names, and threw poorly made pottery at him. "This is the way we must live, and you know that if we venture outside the cave, that bad things will happen! Very bad things...Staying in our cave is the only way to live!"

Finally, one of them suggested that perhaps Boogie was evil, and he should leave the cave, as he no longer belonged. The others loved this idea and intensified their jeering because Boogie's wondering threatened everything they had come to accept. Hurt and scared, Boogie ran from his tribe, out into the world.

As Boogie ran, tears blurred his vision, but he kept running. Eventually, he stopped and rubbed the tears from his eyes. What he saw made him gasp aloud: "Oh, wow!"

The outside world was more beautiful than he could have imagined. No dragon or giant god was waiting to kill him, and it wasn't an expanse of nothingness. The animals were even more impressive and majestic than their shadows could ever have suggested. There was so much more colour, life, and wonder. And the smell! Boogie could never have known there was anything that didn't smell like many people living together in a cave for years on end.

As Boogie looked around, he saw a woman sitting on a hilltop. She also saw him and beckoned him over. As he got closer, he saw that she was ancient, much older than anyone in the cave had been.

The woman introduced herself as The Seer of Truth and Purveyor of Wisdom Who Sits on the Mountainside, or simply, Farah. Farah correctly guessed that Boogie had come from a cave and wondered if he had emerged alone or had brought anyone with him.

Boogie sadly but proudly said he had come alone and wondered where Farah's cave was. Farah explained that she grew up in a time before people lived in caves. Once, people lived together freely in the fields and mountains. Boogie was amazed that people could have once lived outside their caves, let alone with people from other tribes.

Farah began to tell Boogie the story of how people came to live their isolated, sheltered existences in caves.

"When the people lived together in this land, every year, the population grew larger. One year, people began to panic that there would be too many people and insufficient resources to sustain them. So, the elders suggested they build tall towers to survey the surrounding land and see what would be needed to best live off the land.

The people all agreed that this was an excellent idea, and two separate groups formed to build two different towers. Several weeks later, the tribe reconvened. One group declared beyond doubt that the only way to survive was to begin making spears, traps, and tools for hunting. The other group scoffed and guffawed and rolled their eyes and said that, as a community, they needed baskets and storehouses for gathering food and weaving looms to make tents. This quickly escalated into an argument between the two groups, ultimately resulting in the tribe fragmenting into smaller tribes."

Boogie was confused. Why had they disagreed so strongly? Perhaps it was like the shadows on the wall back in the cave; people thought they knew what they saw but didn't have the whole picture.

Farah led Boogie to a tall, ancient tower facing to the east. Farah led Boogie to the top of the tower. As he looked out, Boogie saw a rough, rocky land below, inhabited by buffalo, elk, and sheep. He understood why some of his ancestors thought that spears and traps for hunting were the best way forward.

As Boogie wondered what buffalo might taste like, Farah led him to another old tower, this time facing west. This time, Boogie climbed to the top and saw lush fields and rolling hills covered in berries, grapevines, fruit trees, and wild cotton bushes.

Boogie then understood why the ancestors, who saw the world from this tower, would have thought that baskets, storehouses, and weaving looms were the best way to look after their people.

But why didn't each faction go up the other's tower so they could understand why they each saw differently?

Farah shook her head sadly, "Although that seems simple, it seldom works that way. Instead, people divide and work against each other, defending their views. Why do you think this happens?"

Boogie furrowed his brow. Why had his own tribe chased him from his cave when he questioned their long-held beliefs about the world outside the cave? His eyes grew wide as he realised it was just like his ancestors long ago, unable to listen to and understand others' points of view. This takes courage too. Boogie felt a sudden urge to spread his newly found enlightenment with the others.

"Be careful, Boogie," said Farah. "Remember how painful it was for a curious cave folk like you to leave the cave. Imagine how much harder it will be for others who are satisfied to stay. There are thousands of cave people living in thousands of caves. It will be challenging work to reach all of them."

"Others won't be satisfied once they know of this big world," said Boogie enthusiastically. "They will want to learn more and see it for themselves." Boogie smiled and bade Farah farewell. Farah wished him luck and asked him to bring others back to talk with her so she could share the story of the towers with them.

Boogie started back to his cave with a newfound determination to share what he now knew with his cave-folk. He knew they must learn to see the whole, not just parts and shadows. To do this, they needed to learn to see things from each other's point of view, listen, and explore new ideas together without fear...

Lessons from the fable

The story of Boogie and the cave people has many lessons for us. It suggests that how we view the world can be a distortion of reality, and it explores Boogie's leadership of himself and others. It also illustrates how people react when we challenge deeply held beliefs and assumptions about how they see the world. It challenges us all to consider if what we perceive is reality because our own perspectives are limited or incomplete and influenced by what we think we are seeing. It is a small story with big lessons.

The fable and mental models

The fable also introduces us to mental models, a concept Peter Senge popularised in 1994 in his seminal systems thinking book, *The Fifth Discipline*. Awareness of mental models is one of the five disciplines that he identified as necessary for an organisation to be able to adapt and learn. You may think that all organisations are capable of learning – but are they? In conversations with people within larger organisations, I have discovered that a common challenge is learning from what has already happened and making the necessary changes to respond to that learning. Why is this follow-through so difficult?

There is more than one reason, but the one I will discuss now is in the realm of the Personal, as described in Figure 1. It's about how we humans function psychologically. We all develop heuristics or shortcuts to understand and operate in the world. Our brains take shortcuts to reduce the complexity of life. These shortcuts are sometimes called mental models – or deep unconscious assumptions or beliefs about how the world works.

What is a mental model?

It's like a lens through which you look at things –the lens itself determines what you see and how you interpret what you see. In other words, you often only see what you expect to see – like Boogie's cave people did. The renowned American psychologist Abraham Maslow (who also developed the concept of self-actualisation) said, "for a man who has only a hammer, everything looks like a nail." A mental model can be like the hammer!

For example, you may associate all authority figures with fear based on your life experiences (maybe even within your family as you grew up). This may cause you to retreat from saying what you really want to say to such a person – even though this person has never done anything to warrant your underlying fear. The mental model you hold may be expressed as "authority figures are to be respected" or "authority figures should not be questioned". Either way, your mental model means that you have an expectation about what authority is and does – and sometimes you may even read into what they do the very thing you expect to see. Or your words and actions, shaped by what you expect, may draw out of that person the very behaviour your mental model predicted –so your mental model can become a self-fulfilling prophecy.

Stereotyping is one form of a mental model. Consider the stereotype of all young people being computer savvy or all older people being

computer illiterate. How could these stereotypes cause difficulties in the workplace?

Another way of understanding mental models is to recognise them as an unconscious belief about people and/or situations. For example, one person may view a bright new open-plan office and infer that this means the "management of this organisation is open and accessible – egalitarian". Another may look at the layout and assume that "this is an office in which no one is trusted!"– because management can see what you are doing – all the time. These different ways of looking at things represent the different mental models of how the world works. Maybe both these perceptions can be true at the same time...

Summing up, a mental model is:

- an abstraction (an idea) about how a specific part of the world works.

- a simplification of that specific part of the world that may have been true in a specific example at a point in time and that has been generalised.

- only a model (or assumption or belief) that you think is true – and is not necessarily true – it is incomplete.

Advantages and disadvantages of mental models

We humans have evolved employing mental models and this way of functioning holds benefits for us. Firstly, by generalising about how the world works, we can focus on the thing(s) that seems more important and not use valuable brain power reprocessing the same thing, over and over. For example, driving a car becomes routine with practice and routines can be comfortable and a valuable source of order. We create many daily routines and thinking habits as we employ mental models. Secondly, mental models enable us to make an inference or predict what may happen.

But mental models can have a huge disadvantage too. They influence what we choose to take notice of based upon what the particular mental model indicates is important or what may be expected. So, they may limit what we 'see'. In the earlier fable, Boogie was unable to convince his fellow cave dwellers to examine the mental models they held about the shadows on the walls. The shadows offered limited data of what life may be like outside the cave – but the mental model meant that other data was ignored. The shadows are a metaphor for the mental models or unconscious beliefs the cave people held about the outside world.

Try our new range of Mental Models!

Mental models as thinking habits

Mental models are a form of habitual thinking. Your brain is made up of neural networks or pathways that become stronger the more you use a particular way of thinking. To understand this more easily, imagine a new way of thinking – a new neural network – as a track in the bush, and the more often you use that track, the deeper and wider it becomes. You use it more and more, and it starts to become a dirt road. Use it more, and it develops into a highway. It then becomes so easy to stick to travelling the highway that you find it difficult to 'go off-road', to take a new bush track and travel (think) in a different way.

Our brains also work by association, so another way we can fall into making assumptions is just by association – not thinking it through at all. For example, if we talked about Valentine's Day and then I asked you to think of a colour... how many people would say "red"? Sometimes, just the rhythm of life and work means we get into the habit of seeing and doing things a certain way. The children's game of

Simon Says lures the brain into a pattern and rhythm – life and work can be like that sometimes too. Can you think of times when you are just on 'automatic pilot' because of past patterns and rhythms? I wonder if your team meetings fall into this category.

Airing your mental models

How can we assess whether a mental model is serving us well? The first step is to become aware of the mental models you are using. This shifts them from unconscious to conscious ways of thinking – Peter Senge talks about 'exposing our mental models to the air' or the light of day because if they remain unconscious, the mental model remains 'in the dark'.

The next step is to stop and ask different questions – is this really how the world works? Or is it an assumption that worked well in times gone by but is no longer true? It may be an assumption that you inherited from your parents or family. It may be an assumption that worked well within your family's specific cultural context. It may be an assumption that worked well in your organisation 20 years ago – but not now.

How do you develop the observer in you so that you can more often have your thoughts as opposed to your thoughts having you? What is real, and what is just a belief inside your head?

Mental models and adaptability

Developing the capability to become aware of your own mental models, question them and even decide to change them is the source of your own adaptability as a person. Improving your capability to adapt will enhance your resilience and wellbeing, too, because you will be more able to respond to different circumstances in different ways – you will see different opportunities. Another way of expressing this is to say that you will broaden your bandwidth.

Reflections and Fieldwork

1. Reviewing the fable, what are the key points or lessons that this story conveys to you? What does it take to collaborate and bring different perspectives together?

_____

_____

_____

_____

_____

2. How do these lessons relate to your life and your work today? For example, in what ways are you like Boogie, or Farah or the cave-folk?

_____

_____

_____

_____

_____

3. How is this story relevant to your team and/or organisation currently? Do different parts of your organisation act like different tribes of cave-folk living in different caves?

_____

_____

_____

_____

4. Recall a time when you last stepped out of your comfort zone and listened deeply to understand another person's different and challenging perspective.

- How did it feel?

- In what ways did you have to manage yourself?

- What strategies did you usefully employ?

- What mental models do you think may have been operating for you and the other person?

_____

_____

_____

_____

_____

5. Over the coming week, can you 'catch' yourself employing a mental model? Try to identify when you are operating out of habit based on a deeply held unconscious assumption or belief (mental model). Were you successful in identifying a mental model – bringing it to the surface and exposing it to the air? How did you become aware of it? What happened as a result? What have you learned about this specific mental model? Is it serving you well, or is it time to explore an alternative?

_____

_____

_____

_____

_____

CHAPTER 3

Feeling bad?

Maybe you are thinking bad!

Questions addressed in the chapter:

- How can you experience a happier and more satisfying life and work life?

- How can you influence more positive relationships with others?

- What personal beliefs (mental models) may be getting in your way?

Have you ever experienced a time when you felt quite calm or even excited, and this state was crushed by a message, text, or email from someone else? Maybe that person was someone you were having a difficult time with...

Observing our own stories and their impact

A colleague once shared the story of how she spent an entire day worrying about a meeting with her line manager. The manager had caught her on her way into the office and asked her to stop by the manager's office at the end of the day.

This colleague built a whole story in her head about what the request meant. "I'm in trouble", "What have I done wrong?" "This person is never satisfied." All these thoughts raced through her head all day, and as she approached the manager's office, she noticed how stressed, anxious and generally bad she was feeling. She also noticed how she was beginning to construct defences for herself - she was not feeling open and willing to collaborate.

(It is interesting to note that when we feel stressed or in a lower state of mind, we are less able to collaborate with others. We become quite closed off and narrowly focussed – the range of opportunities seems to close.)

It turned out that the manager just wanted help with an IT problem and had heard that my friend had some expertise in this area! All that worrying was for nothing, and an otherwise good day spoiled for my friend. Have you experienced something similar?

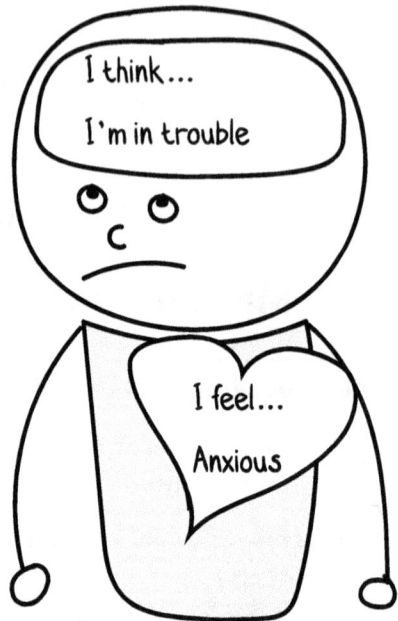

A fellow coach once observed, "If you are feeling bad, you are thinking bad!" And that sums up what psychology teaches us about the relationship between our thinking and emotions – they are interrelated and feed off each other. They are also interrelated with our beliefs (mental models) about people and circumstances. Our thoughts, emotions, unconscious beliefs and assumptions combine to generate the stories that we tell ourselves. The stories may seem real – but they probably are not the whole truth.

Being aware of this relationship is very important if you want to improve your own experience of life and work. Who doesn't want to feel good?

Experiencing all our emotions is healthy

By saying "If you are feeling bad, you are thinking bad" I don't mean to imply that if you are feeling down because of a recent separation from a loved one or a death in the family, that you should ignore those feelings or that they are in any way bad. Life does deal us these situations, and it is not healthy to suppress anger, grief, or sadness.

Expressing them is important, and the upcoming exercise regarding mental models, and how we feel about expressing negative emotions may be helpful.

Benefits of nurturing positive emotions

Positive emotions are more than just feeling happy. Positive emotions include optimism, curiosity, joy, love, compassion, appreciation, gratitude, and amusement. Positive emotions are also the crucible of enhanced outcomes because they influence how we:

- interact with and collaborate with others

- spot opportunities around us

- persist when the going gets tough

- solve problems.

If you can cultivate a positive state of mind in yourself and experience positive emotions, you will be someone whom others seek out for your empathetic listening and advice and someone whom others enjoy working with.

Recognising your emotions, managing them, and healthily expressing them are central to productive and happy relationships and good outcomes.

How to deliberately experience positive emotions more often

There are two types of strategies you can put into place to help you feel more positive (or sustain a more positive/higher state of mind).

The first is longer term and involves taking better care of yourself physically and spiritually to help increase your baseline sense of wellbeing and resilience. These self-care strategies include examining your patterns of:

1. Nutrition

2. Exercise

3. Sleep

4. Being in nature

5. Connecting with others

6. Leisure activities

7. Experiencing music

The second class of strategies are shorter-term and can be employed at a moment's notice. One model[1] I teach is:

- Notice when you may be thinking/feeling sad, tired, stressed, anxious, frustrated, worried, angry, hopeless, depressed, or resigned.

- Shift your state of mind by employing a deep breathing technique, listening to music, or getting some sunshine. I recommend and teach the Heart Math Institute's 'Coherent Breathing Technique'. Using this technique will help you lift your state of mind to feeling, for example, calm, content, relaxed, energised or even passionate.

- Own your lower state of mind if you cannot shift it (and sometimes we just can't) and don't allow your negative emotions to become contagious to others – explain and ask for your colleagues' support instead.

Mental models about emotions

Employing this approach also requires us to examine our mental models about emotions and how we might express them. Becoming aware of these can help us improve our own wellbeing by developing a better relationship with the full range of our emotions – both positive and negative.

Like many of our mental models, beliefs about having and expressing emotions are often learned from our parents, grandparents, siblings, and teachers, who learned the same lessons but perhaps in a different

---

1   *This technique summarised by Alexander Caillet in an online video available at https://www.youtube.com/watch?v=bTk92sr0mZE*

context. Perhaps those beliefs served them well in their time and context, but today's world is changing, and that's a good reason to revisit these beliefs and determine if the same beliefs are still serving you well.

How do we notice emotions in others?

Becoming more familiar with our own emotions helps with observing and decoding the emotions of others and is part of Emotional Intelligence (EQ). Noticing emotions in others assists us in nurturing positive relationships, which are so important to our wellbeing. But how do we notice emotions?

Listening to people is more than listening to words. We can register the emotions people are expressing by observing facial expressions and body language closely, listening carefully to the tone of their voice, the pace they are speaking at, and the type of language they are using. We can also choose to focus on what is not being said. Overall, we are trying to gauge whether there is a congruence between what is said and what is being conveyed in other ways through non-verbal communication. Noticing this congruence or non-congruence can be a way of beginning a deeper conversation about what people are really thinking and trying to say. And isn't that what a healthy relationship is about?

In your workplace, it may be appropriate to talk about psychological safety and developing a team culture where people feel safe to say what they think (in a constructive manner). Here are some useful questions to discuss in your team:

1. Do people always say what they think? How do we know if they are not saying what they believe?

2. Why might someone not assert themselves and say what they think? Is being assertive the same as being aggressive?

How can we nurture an environment in which people feel comfortable to be themselves and can offer their suggestions and opinions safely?

Reflections and Fieldwork:

1. Recall a recent incident where you ended up 'thinking bad and feeling bad'. Practice applying some of the ideas in this chapter and develop a strategy for how you could turn that story around. Or if you did manage to turn it around, how did you do it? Did your actions reflect and maybe add to the concepts described above?

_____

_____

_____

_____

_____

_____

_____

_____

_____

_____

2. Practice noticing how you feel before you meet to collaborate with others. Do you notice a pattern in your emotions? What did you learn about attempting to shift your state of mind if you need to? What works for you?

_____

_____

_____

_____

_____

_____

_____

_____

3. Consider your mental models about expressing negative emotions at work.... And at home. Are they different? Why?

_____

_____

_____

_____

_____

_____

_____

_____

_____

4. Practice listening and observing emotions in others. What do you notice about your ability to notice and understand emotions in other people?

_____

_____

_____

_____

_____

_____

_____

_____

_____

_____

CHAPTER 4

You've got talent (strengths)!

Questions addressed in the chapter:

- **What are strengths?**

- **How can you identify your strengths?**

- **How can you spot other people's strengths?**

- **What are the benefits of working to your strengths?**

- **What is 'flow', and how can you cultivate the conditions for it more often?**

Our modern culture seems very focused on appreciating the talent of singers, film stars and sports identities, but we are less quick to appreciate our own talents. In fact, many people think they do not have any talent at all. I believe you have talents, or strengths as they are becoming known. Identifying your strengths and learning how to work with them more each day will not only improve how well you do your job but also how satisfied and positive you feel as a result of doing your work. It's one way to become more of who you already are (or engage with the process of self-actualisation as described by Abraham Maslow).

What is a talent or strength?

When I talk about 'strengths', I mean not only things that you are naturally good at, or have become good at, but also things that make you *feel*

strong when you do them – it's as if you were somehow meant to be doing them. A strength is simply a combination of personal qualities you were born with or that have developed in you. It means that when you use these qualities it feels effortless, and when you apply your strengths, you consistently perform at a high level. Because you are drawn to do these things, use these strengths, you usually practice doing them. And practice improves performance. You may also have learned some more skills to layer over the top of your strength, but the strength was there before you learned the skills. So, skills are not the same as strengths – but are often associated with them.

Why is it that we are often unaware of the strengths or talents we have?

Identifying strengths is a relatively new area of exploration in helping people to develop themselves, improve their performance at work, and generate more satisfying careers and work experiences. The notion of strengths emerged from the new field of positive psychology as recently as the 1980s. Marcus Buckingham is a researcher and author about strengths and employee engagement who first published in the 1990s. He has been influential in growing the conversation about strengths. But there are still mental models at work that sound a bit like this:

- We all need to be well-rounded people and that means being good enough at everything so as not to let the side down – that is, it means eliminating weaknesses.

- People grow the most in the areas of their weaknesses.

- Good line managers will point out your weaknesses to help you improve your performance.

You can probably add to this list from your own experiences. The point is that these are mental models. They may be true in specific cases, for example, where the weakness really is holding back your career progression, but they are not universally true. There are several structures and beliefs in our organisations that still reflect these mental models:

- Performance reviews that identify 'opportunities for improvement'.

- A focus on providing 'feedback' (not usually about what you did spectacularly well).

- Drilling down on problems.

Positive psychology has contributed to changing the ways in which we develop and grow our people. By focusing on strengths and helping people to use their strengths more often, employee engagement and satisfaction increase. Focusing on what we do well and finding ways to do more of it may be a new idea for some because, for a long time, our culture has focused on weaknesses and problems. As we know, what we focus on grows, which may be why discovering and working with your strengths is not as familiar to you as it might be.

Another explanation lies in understanding that your strengths are natural to you – you didn't have to learn how to do these things, so it's very likely you don't notice them as anything special and assume that everyone can do things like this. That is not true – it's a myth, but because we haven't thought about it much, that is often what we believe.

Let's illustrate what strengths are with a couple of stories.

Steve is a builder, but he doesn't like building new homes, he likes to transform something that already is, into something new. He has big ideas and loves to chat and 'blue sky' with people. He has a way of linking ideas together and seeing patterns so that he can form a new insight. He is likeable with a keen sense of optimism. Steve's key strength is his ability to envision what could be. He could do this all day and never feel tired; he does it without effort and feels invigorated when he is doing it. Envisioning just happens for him. He also does it exceedingly well every time. Steve's strength is also best seen within a specific context – transforming something that is into something new.

Rachel is a great sales assistant. She loves dressing people up and always has since she was two years old and first refused to wear what her mother put out for her. Rachel has style and flair in how she dresses and seems somehow to know what people look best in. She is a people person - outgoing and curious about others. She makes new best friends wherever she goes. These two things combined mean she just loves helping people find the right outfit. She will spend all day helping someone find what's perfect for them, and her customers know that she would never give them misleading advice. Her strengths in forming good rapport and trusting relationships with individual people, combined with her flair for style and design in clothes, means she tops the sales list every week in her department at work. And she never tires of it. She comes home more charged than she goes to work most days.

How do you identify your strengths?

Marcus Buckingham suggests there are some tell-tale signs, and these are:

- You look forward to and eagerly anticipate times when you will use your strengths.

- When you use your strengths, you become engrossed and focused and may lose track of time, becoming easily immersed in the task at hand. You complete the task to an exceedingly high standard of work – every time.

- When you have finished, you feel better than when you started… using your strengths is psychologically energising, not draining.

You can use the questions at the end of this chapter to help you reveal your own strengths. Additionally, there are online assessments you can undertake. Two assessments that I recommend are:

- The Clifton Strengths Finder (named after Donald O. Clifton, one of the 'fathers of strengths psychology' at Gallup organisation) identifies 34 major strengths themes and is available at a small cost online.

- VIA Character Strengths Inventory (developed from the research by positive psychologist, Martin Seligman). VIA was originally shorthand for Values in Action Inventory, and this inventory can be undertaken for free at the VIA Institute on Character website.

If you explore both these strengths assessments, you will notice that they define 'strengths' slightly differently. You will also notice a connection to your values. I discuss values in chapter 5.

Satisfaction and Being 'In Flow'

There are benefits that emerge from understanding your strengths and designing your workday with your team leader or manager, to enable you to employ your strengths more and more. These benefits include:

- Creating career pathways that are satisfying to you

- Improving performance at work

- Nurturing more creativity or seeds for innovation

Additionally, research into creativity indicates that when people use their strengths in fields of endeavour that they are also passionate about, they will be more persistent in the endeavour and more creative in their problem-solving. This has got to be of major interest to most organisations today. These results are also echoed in the concept of 'flow'.

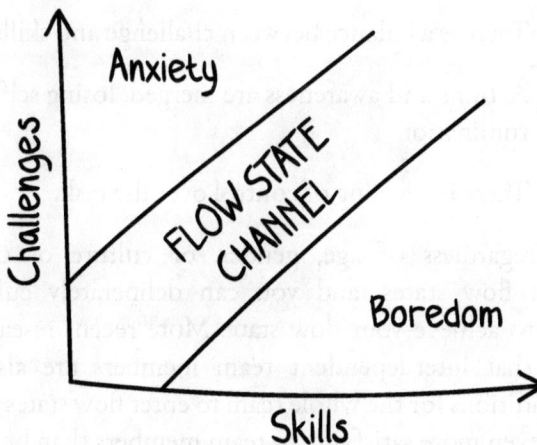

Figure 3: The flow state channel

45

Mihaly Csikszentmihalyi is another of the co-founders of positive psychology, and he was the first to research the flow state. You have heard about sports people who identify and talk about being 'in the zone'. This is the same as the flow state. Flow occurs when your skill level corresponds with the challenge with which you are engaged. Csikszentmihalyi was interested in how to cultivate happiness, and his interviews with athletes, musicians and artists were designed to understand when they experienced optimal performance levels and how they felt when they were engaged in these experiences. He coined the term 'flow state' because so many of these people described how their work just 'flowed out of them'. He found that flow is essential for a productive employee and imperative for a well-satisfied, engaged, and contented worker.

Csikszentmihalyi describes eight characteristics of flow:

- Complete concentration on the task

- Clarity of goals and rewards in mind and immediate feedback

- Transformation of time (speeding up/slowing down)

- The experience is intrinsically rewarding

- Effortlessness and ease

- There is a balance between challenge and skills

- Actions and awareness are merged, losing self-conscious rumination

- There is a feeling of control over the task.

Everyone, regardless of age, gender, or culture of origin, has experienced flow states, and you can deliberately cultivate the conditions to achieve your flow state. More recent research is also suggesting that interdependent team members are also able to nurture conditions for the whole team to enter flow states together – and that is even more satisfying to team members than being in flow on their own.

Reflections and Fieldwork:

1. With someone who knows you well, explain what strengths are and ask them what they think your strengths are. Listen carefully and ask questions to find out more and more specific examples of your strengths as this person views them.

   The real test, however, is running these examples through the three points under the heading 'How do you find out what your strengths are?' Earlier in this chapter. People may see you doing things well – but it is you who will know what your energy levels are like before, during and after... so only you can really say which are strengths and which are not. You may be very good at something that you don't enjoy! List what you learn are your top 3 - 5 strengths.

   _____

   _____

   _____

   _____

   _____

2. Take notice of the tasks you do over the next 2 weeks. Try writing down the things that you really look forward to doing and those that you actively avoid. Become more attuned to what these things are and how the circumstances that surround them may influence your appreciation of the task

   _____

   _____

   _____

   _____

   _____

3. Now that you are more aware of what your strengths are, consider how can you organise your work to use your strengths more often. Is there someone else in your team who has a strength in an area that you do not? How could you reallocate work to make better use of people's strengths?

_____

_____

_____

_____

_____

_____

_____

4. Think of a time when you were really engaged with your work. A time when you looked up and found you had missed lunch or worked right through the afternoon. A time when you accomplished a task without any difficulty or distractions. When you were really in FLOW. What conditions enabled you to achieve this state at that time? Consider the type of work, the time of day, who else was around, how you were managed etc.

_____

_____

_____

_____

_____

_____

_____

CHAPTER 5

You've also got passion and purpose

Questions addressed in this chapter:

- **What do we mean by values?**

- **How do values develop, and do they change?**

- **What might be the relationship between strengths, values, and a sense of meaning and purpose?**

- **How can you connect your values to your organisation's values?**

Strengths are important ways to get the things you think are important done... but how do you decide what is important enough to do?

Your decisions are strongly influenced by what you value.

About values

What you value could be seen to be partly determined by your personality preferences – so you may prefer to work in an orderly way or an unstructured way (opposite ends of the spectrum), depending upon how you are naturally predisposed. So, if you like order and structure I would say that you are someone who values these qualities. (And there is a link back to your strengths here too, you may also have a strength that is about organisation, or logical, linear thinking or well-ordered and structured instructions.)

In addition to this, your life experiences, how and even where you were raised as a child, what your parents thought was important, how influential people in your life affected you, the best and the worst experiences at home, school, and work, have all taught you lessons about what is important. They give you a sense of what is right and wrong or what 'should' be. What you value is related to what you think is good, important, useful, beautiful, or desirable. Values are essentially beliefs that you have been taught, and so there are also links to the topic of mental models. This can be a very challenging idea. If your values are not what defines you as your authentic self, then who are you?

What you value is also contextual. That is, it is dependent upon the situation you are in and the type of role that you may be fulfilling. Roles such as child, sibling, partner, parent, sports team member, worker, manager, business owner, carer, activist, etc. We have learned lessons or beliefs or mental models about how to be a 'good child' or a 'good worker' and these may become values we hold in these situations and roles.

Some theories of personal development also suggest that as we grow and mature or develop as people through life, what we value also changes. So as a child, who is naturally self-centred, we may value getting our own way but as an adult, we may value collaboration over self-interest.

Triggers and needs

'Needing' introduces another distinction that often confuses any discussion about values. Values are desirable and things we are naturally drawn to – so they are usually positively energising and, in this way, are like employing your strengths. But when you need something beyond your own resources - that is, when you become 'needy' or dependent rather than interdependent to function, then it is often a drain on your energy, and it can draw you away from doing the things you value.

For example, your sense of well-being may depend on your feeling or thinking that your actions are approved of by other people and this need may keep you from displaying your value of speaking your truth. If you can identify the 'needs' that make you dependent and raise your awareness of them enough so that they no longer overwhelm your actions, you can move into the space of your actions being guided more and more by what you value – which is more positively energising.

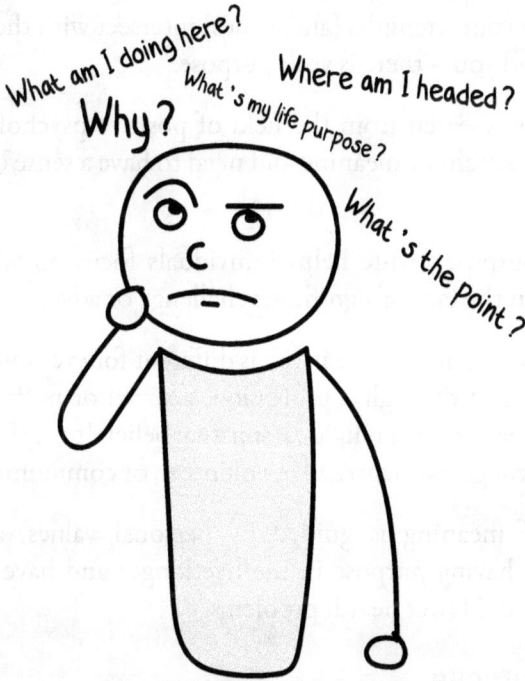

What am I doing here?
Why?
What's my life purpose?
Where am I headed?
What's the point?

Values, passion, and purpose

As you are guided more by what you value, you may find yourself starting to stand up for what you value. This lies at the very heart of becoming who you really are.

Depending upon the level of energy you have for something you value, you may be described as passionate. Passion is neither positive nor negative – it is just an intense emotion. Passionate people may love – or kill. But generally, we think of passion as a positive quality – it is certainly a source of energy to take specific actions.

Passion founded on values is an uplifting and positive experience. If you can combine your emotion with your reason (emotional intelligence), then you have a foundation for a life (and work) that is energising and meaningful.

Aristotle (a philosopher from ancient Greece who also taught Alexander the Great), said, "Where your talents and the needs of the world meet, there lies your vocation." We can update this and say, "Where your strengths (and values) intersect with the important needs around you – there is your purpose."

Modern day research from the field of positive psychology reveals that people search for meaning and need to have a sense of value and worth[2].

Having a purpose in life helps individuals focus on what is truly important in the face of significant challenge or adversity.

Having meaning or purpose in life is different for everyone. Meaning may be pursued through a profession, a social or political cause, a creative endeavour, or a religious/spiritual belief. It may be found in a career or through extracurricular, volunteer, or community activities.

A sense of meaning is guided by personal values, and people who report having purpose in life live longer and have greater life satisfaction and fewer health problems.

Shared purpose

Many people feel overwhelmed by the idea of having or identifying a purpose. We can remove some of the pressure by realising that because our context changes during our lifetime and as we move from one situation to another, it makes sense that our purposes (like our values) may reprioritise too. (I will return to purpose a few more times in this book.)

Purpose is often interpreted as an individual's big goal – but as we recognise our interconnectedness with others, we begin to realise that focussing just on 'my purpose', 'what I want as an individual' is limiting and lacks connection with the very people involved in the challenge you care about. Also, if your well-being is enhanced by working on issues bigger than you, then a shared purpose may achieve that more readily than an individual one.

---

2   *Seligman M., 2011, Flourish, Random House, Sydney*

Values do reprioritise and we adapt

Over time and in different circumstances, we all reprioritise our values. As times change and we need to change with them, we face the adaptive challenge of deciding to let go of some old ways of expressing what's most important. Because these values or beliefs were often learned from people who were and are precious to us, letting go can be difficult. We may feel like we are letting that important person down. It can take time to negotiate this transition and it is a path often described as two steps forward and one back. Be gentle with yourself – you can do it. Asking for help from others and putting in some type of system to help you move ahead is easier than going it alone.

For example, the need to be more aware of my health has become clear since COVID-19.

To implement my self-care transition, I needed to reprioritise my values. The internal adaptation I needed to make was, "I matter and need to come first' after years of being a mum where, "kids matter most, and I can wait." So, with the support of my family, and some professional advice, I have begun a regime of exercise, healthy eating, and awareness of my own needs and I am feeling the benefits.

There is an important principle at the heart of this example. All my work has confirmed that difficult change (individual and collective) tends to happen best when our focus is not on what we want to leave behind or 'let go' of, but on something we want to move towards. We are motivated to change not so much by what is wrong with the way things are, as by a vision of how we really want things to be. The 'letting go' happens spontaneously when we are drawn towards something preferable.

Sometimes we choose to reprioritise and on other occasions life makes us adapt. COVID-19, the climate related fires and floods... These outside forces and our context (life) will ensure we change when we need to – it's simply a matter of how long before we get the message!

Connection to corporate values

A lot of time is often invested in developing a list of corporate values because senior managers recognise the importance of values in decision making, taking action, and nurturing culture. Announcing the values is the easy bit – living them consistently is the difficult part. Indeed, in nearly every organisation I work within, people tell me that management does not live the values. There is an inconsistency between the espoused values and the lived values.

The first challenge is an ongoing adaptive challenge – doing what we intend. But it is also complicated by changing contexts. The top 5 values in the strategic plan or vision document are often not contextualised very strongly. Given this lack of context, it's not surprising that decisions are made that highlight different values in different circumstances and so confuse others with an apparent lack of consistency.

The second problem of 'aligning everyone behind the values' is a misunderstanding – of both the desired outcome and the process required. The desired outcome should be to connect team members to the values in ways that enable them to identify their own values in the corporate values. They need to make sense of the corporate values and connect to them.

Different processes are available to do this – the one I favour involves everyone in the initial process of developing the list of values. How are the corporate values identified? Whose values are they? Who decides what the corporation values? Is the focus really on values, or are the stated values proxies for behaviours that senior management would like to see more of? Are the corporate values expressions of what is most important for us? Involving everyone in the initial conversations will provide answers to these questions and connect all stakeholders with the values identified.

Providing opportunities for staff to contribute to the shaping of the corporate values and to discuss what that means in their work is another process to support the team to embrace the values of the strategic plan or vision.

Reflections and Fieldwork:

1. If your values are not what defines you as your 'authentic self' then who are you?

_____

_____

_____

2. The context matters and while the things you value most may endure, the values that are most relevant to you at any time depend upon the context. So, what are the values you express each day, within your context? Dr John Demartini has been researching values for four decades and has developed the Value Determination Process. With 13 questions, the process helps you identify and determine the hierarchy of your values.

   At the time of writing, the process is free online at: https://drdemartini.com/values/

3. Extending this line of thinking, and considering the challenges in the world around you (as proposed by Aristotle) what is your purpose at this time? How does this relate to your current work? How could it relate more to your current work and your life? (This purpose doesn't have to be a lifetime commitment, it's just your sense of purpose now and it can be quite small. At my mother's funeral, I discovered her sense of purpose was to make others feel remembered and cared for by her small gifts of bouquets of flowers that were delivered over many years to various friends at times of difficulty.)Extending this line of thinking, and considering the challenges in the world around you (as proposed by Aristotle) what is your purpose at this time? How does this relate to your current work? How could it relate more to your current work and your life?

_____

_____

_____

_____

_____

4. Try drawing a mind map that reflects your strengths, values, needs – and your purpose. This is a tough assignment, but have a go at it. It can be fun just spending time with a pencil or some coloured pens and drawing and thinking at the same time. There is something about the tactile nature of pen and paper that allows ideas to emerge as you go. Just start – and see what happens. Use a big piece of paper, to give your mind the freedom to explore. Spend some time reflecting on your values and finding the connections to organisational values within the context of your day-to-day work and team. Once again, drawing can be helpful in making these connections.

5. Spend some time reflecting on your values and finding the connections to organisational values within the context of your day-to-day work and team. Try listing your values on a sheet of paper along with a list of organisational values on the same sheet. Now draw lines connecting your values to the organisational values. Identify the places you connect.

_____

_____

_____

_____

_____

_____

_____

_____

CHAPTER 6

Leadership – it's not always from a position of authority

Questions addressed in this chapter:

- Why is your leadership required?

- What is the nature of the new, emerging leadership?

- Do you need permission to exercise your leadership?

This chapter explores two related ideas. The first is that we are all interconnected... and that because of this we can take conscious responsibility for making 'the system' work. We can all exercise leadership. When we care about something enough to exercise our leadership, we automatically assume some responsibility for it.

Everything is connected, and you are influencing all the time

When I start working within organisations and communities, I often see evidence of a particular shared mindset or mental model. There is a sense that the organisation is like a piece of machinery that either works on its own or is controlled by someone else. Or perhaps the sense is that each of us might keep one wheel turning, but someone else designs and builds the machine...and decides what each wheel does and how it's connected (or not) to the rest of the machine. Somehow people think of themselves as separate from and not responsible for the organisation's workings – it's someone else's job!

This assumption of separation is one of the deeply entrenched but unconscious mental models that is now being challenged by scientists through quantum physics and biology and the study of living systems. Through these research fields, scientists have been revealing how deeply interconnected everything is – especially in what we call complex or living systems. Such living systems are natural and can be found in weather, environment, economy and social systems like beehives, ant nests, human organisations, and communities.

No doubt, you have felt our interconnectedness through past events like the Global Financial Crisis and, more recently, through the COVID-19 pandemic, climate events (like the fire, floods and droughts occurring across Australia and the world), and political upheaval everywhere. All these events highlight our interconnectedness. We notice that events in a distant location impact us quickly and strongly.

If we believe that we are separate from the world around us, then it makes sense that someone else is in control of the workings, but if we are active participants in it – interconnected – then we are also influencing, naturally, how the world works. Our connectedness means that we automatically share a capacity and a responsibility for keeping the world and our organisations unchanged or helping to change them – to make a difference.

Do you often think about how your specific day-to-day actions impact the lives and outcomes of others? Not many of us do. For example, if you really thought about it, you might see the indirect, small but none-the-less real link between your decision to drive your car each day (increasing atmospheric levels of CO_2 as you go) and changes in climate resulting in reduced snowfall in the Himalayas and reduced melted snow flowing as water into India. This results in children in India spending more time walking to collect water for their families. Closer to home, you might link the CO_2 emissions produced by your decisions with changes in rainfall in our own regional areas of Australia where our food is grown.

What would it mean if you started to think like this? What would be the implications for how you perceive your influence in - and on - the world?

HOLONS IN A HOLARCHY

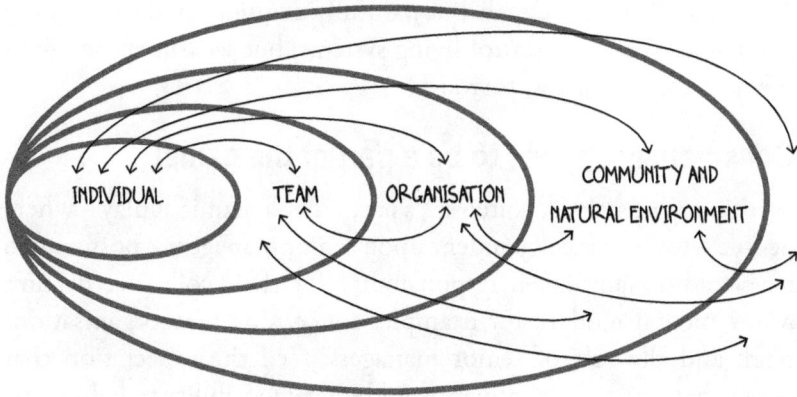

Figure 4: Perceiving and acting with awareness of the whole system

When you see the world in this interconnected way, it is common to initially feel powerless and inconsequential because of the difference in relative sizes. The world, or community, or organisation is big. You are just one person. What can you do that makes a difference?

But if you think a little more... We can see that indeed we do have influence – whether we are consciously aware of it or not. We are a part of all this – not separate from it. Our every choice has an influence, often way beyond what we can see... and like a butterfly beating its wings on one side of the world, you just may create a hurricane on the other side of the world.

Even if we choose not to change things, by doing that we are choosing a certain path that will influence the whole and contribute to maintaining the status quo in the system.

Figure 4 provides an illustration of this way of viewing our relationships with self, others, our organisation and the community and natural environment of which we are all a part. Holons (each egg shape) form a series of nested subsystems within the larger system, which we could think of as our planet Earth. These holons form a holarchy which Arthur Koestler first conceived of as a way of describing the relationships in natural, living systems. The arrows indicate how each holon is influenced by and influences each other holon in the system. It is a dynamic, moving feast! It is an inherently messy, uncertain, unpredictable, and uncontrollable context within which constant learning is required if we are to survive and prosper. This reality has been clearly but painfully demonstrated to us by the pandemic. We can't control living systems, but we can engage with them and learn our way forward.

Consciously choose to be a part of the game!

Within organisations, I often see a particular dynamic at play – where people have become dependent upon senior managers – bosses, who have traditionally taken responsibility for their collective destiny. Many mental models, for example, concerning how organisations work and the role of senior managers, feed the expectation that people have no say, no influence, and no responsibility to help shape the organisational life that they really want.

In fact, Ron Heifetz, a Harvard professor in leadership, suggests there is an unwritten social contract that underpins the 'hero leader' model. Paraphrasing, it is this; "I will follow you and give you authority and power over me, for you to protect me and keep me secure. And if you get it wrong, I can blame you, because you assumed responsibility for me."

But seen through the lens of living systems, it is your right to have and accept responsibility for yourself and for helping to shape the whole system. Compared to many, perhaps most, organisations, this is a substantial shift in 'the way we do things' and is at the heart of the constructive cultural change your organisation may be pursuing through engaging me to work with you.

AUTHORITY ≠ LEADERSHIP

This doesn't mean you assume the role of CEO. Everyone still has their different roles within the organisation to fulfill. It does mean that you can take responsibility for exercising your leadership from wherever you are in the organisation to make things work better and to improve the experience of life at work – you don't have to be 'in charge'.

Your purpose is to participate fully for the greater good

You could think of self-leadership as consciously accepting your personal responsibility to influence the whole by honouring the way everything is connected, both within yourself and between you and the world around you. You exercise your leadership when you set out to influence and learn with others to change the way we see things and how we act.

Some might see that responsibility as an onerous burden to carry. I see it as a source of inspiration and possibility! How great to know that you can influence things and be a part of the game rather than sitting on the sidelines watching others play the game and having all the fun! No more "life of quiet desperation" - you can be in the thick of it, shaping the life you want for yourself and others.

Reflections and Fieldwork:

1. Reflect on one recent experience that illustrates how different elements of your work are connected to other people and even departments.

_____

_____

_____

_____

_____

2. Complete these sentences to reveal different mental models that you may hold about leadership – then discuss them with your team members.

   a. Good leaders...

   _____

   _____

b. Bad leaders...

_____

_____

c. If I choose to influence others or exercise leadership...

_____

_____

3. As you reflect on Figure 4 and the notion that a living system is inherently uncontrollable, what examples can you find in your life and work that bear this statement out?

_____

_____

_____

_____

_____

4. Different organisational positions have different levels of formal authority. How can everyone exercise a leadership role and influence others from different positions? What will it take, or how can you create the conditions, for everyone to be able to contribute fully?

_____

_____

_____

_____

CHAPTER 7

Skill building to collaborate and influence

Questions addressed in this chapter:

- **How can you exercise your leadership?**

- **What skills do you need and how can you develop them?**

- **How can you help generate positive energy for new ways of doing things?**

One of the key skills to exercise your leadership in a way that helps others find their own answers is the art of effective communication. Listening deeply and using your sense of curiosity to ask questions that help other people to learn as they reflect upon their own experiences are skills that you can develop. This practice, which is both art and science, has become known over the past 20-30 years as coaching.

Coaching skills: behaviours of emotional intelligence

A coaching approach pays huge dividends, not just at work but also at home. I have used this approach with my children, and it may be a coincidence, but we didn't endure difficult teenage years and we are all still good friends as the 'kids' move into 30s.

A fundamental principle of employing a coaching approach is that coaching is focused on exploring a topic together to find new answers together. It is not about imposing answers that the coach knew beforehand. New possibilities and answers emerge from the conversation. It is a process of collaborative inquiry and adult learning.

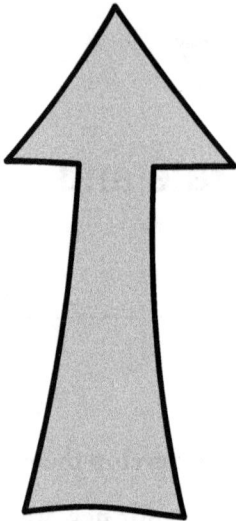

- Awareness
- Sense of Responsiblity

Listening

Listening well is the first step. Can you develop or enhance your ability to listen so well that you get a deep sense of what it is that the other person is trying to say? Can you 'feel' what they are feeling as they talk (even if they don't say anything directly about how they are feeling)? Can you quieten your own mind so that you are not distracted by what you want to say next? Can you listen and then converse with the other person in a way that does not make them feel or think that you have a particular agenda or barrow to push? And because you have cleared your mind and listened so well, can you ask a question that springs from your sense of curiosity – and helps the other person become more aware of the situation they are exploring?

Questions to raise awareness

The reason we usually ask questions is to gather more information so we can make a better decision. The *purpose* of asking questions in a coaching conversation is to help the other person become more aware of different ways of looking at the same thing (airing mental models) and discovering what they are learning about themselves, others, the situation, etc. And as the other person considers these questions, they will likely create new neural pathways and learning. Change is occurring as the two of you converse. From there, it is easy to ask, "What has been the standout thing for you about our conversation?" and follow up with, "So, what will you do about that?" It is as easy as that to catalyse change... and exercise your leadership.

Linking to a context broader than just the workplace, I found the best question for coaching teenagers was, "Tell me specifically what you have planned that means you will remain safe?"

Being purposeful about the process of collaboration

When collaborating with others, we need an agreed process to help everyone think together. One simple process is Sir John Whitmore's GROW agenda which can be employed with individuals or groups. Applied in a group or team setting, the participants develop a shared:

- *Goal* or vision

- Understanding of current *Reality*

- Array of possible *Options* to move forward

- Agreement on what the group *Will* do now, when, and how.

When collaborating, each participant needs to hold their personal purpose very lightly. If each person has a fiercely held personal purpose and vision, then the group will not really collaborate – it will merely be a contest of best ideas being pitched against other best ideas. The attitude each group member could cultivate is one of offering their views to the group and then letting go of them for the group to transform them by adding everyone's perceptions. Noticing and managing the tension between advocating for our views and 'letting go' is a crucial capability to develop.

Collaboration occurs best when the group agrees on the question that they want or need to find an answer to, and all positions of authority are left at the door for the discussion period. Starting with a question that you can treat as a 'straw man' to be torn apart will not polarise the group in the way starting with an answer might. When a community gathers around an issue of concern to all, it begins from the common ground – one of concern without answers in sight yet.

Nurturing the conditions for genuine collaboration requires the very best of those in positions of higher authority. Firstly, because we are asking them to put their answers aside too and begin at the question. It also requires them to be aware of the possible impact of their position of authority and purposefully nurture a human environment in which everyone feels free to speak and contribute without fear of repercussions. It is a very purposeful strategy because nurturing these conditions will allow all participants in the process to:

- contribute their unique perspective on the issue within the system, enabling the group to develop a deeper shared understanding of the issue.

- work through their own thinking and problem-solving (doing their own inner adaptive change work in the process).

- learn together and implement new experiments together to move the issue forward.

Appreciative Inquiry Insight

As I noted when we discussed strengths, a new paradigm has emerged over the last 20 years (it continues to develop but is by no means complete). Part of this paradigm is about understanding how to engage people, and provide the space for them to enthusiastically contribute what they know about what works for them. One of these practices is strengths-based and is known as Appreciative Inquiry.

Appreciative Inquiry developed from work that a young research student was doing in a hospital in the USA, where another student named David Cooperrider was helping. The research was about physician leadership at one of the world's top medical centres – the Cleveland Clinic.

"They asked these leaders to tell the stories of their biggest successes as well as their biggest failures. But when Cooperrider looked at the data, he was drawn only to their success stories. Listening to their [stories] of strength and strong leadership, he was amazed by the level of positive co-operation, innovation, and egalitarian governance at the clinic."[3]

The rest, as they say, is history. Cooperrider went on, with the support of his supervisor and the Clinic's chair, to view the data exclusively looking for the positives. "...everything that served to give life to the system and to people when they were most alive, effective, committed, and empowered. Everything else was considered irrelevant."

The process that was developed is now called Appreciative Inquiry, and it has a worldwide following. It has been proven to catalyse transformational changes within organisations delivering better working conditions and better results.

Appreciative Inquiry (AI) is a process that evolved within an organisational context – that is, its original purpose was to catalyse transformational change in organisations. It is now spreading to community work too – especially in the field of sustainability. AI is both an attitude and a process. The attitude is one based upon the following beliefs:

- People construct the reality they want or think about (this is in line with the often-used quote from Anwar Sadat, "He who cannot change the very fabric of his thought will never be able to change reality.")

- What people focus their attention on grows (so if you think mostly about what's wrong –then that's what you will notice more of – focus on what is working, and that's what you notice more of)

- People have an abundance of resourcefulness and creativity at their disposal – they are 'designed' to be successful.

AI comprises four stages (four D's) and is another simple process that your group or team might employ to help you think things through and make decisions together:

---

3   *Cooperrider, D. L., Whitney, D., & Stavros, J. M. (2008). Appreciative Inquiry Handbook: for leaders of change (2nd ed.). Brunswick, Ohio; Crown Custom Publishing.*

1. Discovery (what gives life?)

    - Where is success evident now? What conditions enable that success?

2. Dream (envisioning what might be)

    - How do we really want to experience [this issue - enter your challenge] when we have successfully resolved it?

3. Design (determining how can it be)

    - As a first step, what needs to change, personally, culturally, and structurally (systems and processes) for us to bring our Dream into being?

4. Destiny (remaining connected to each other to create what will be)

    - When and how will we remain connected and keep our Dream lively as we learn more about bringing the Dream into being?

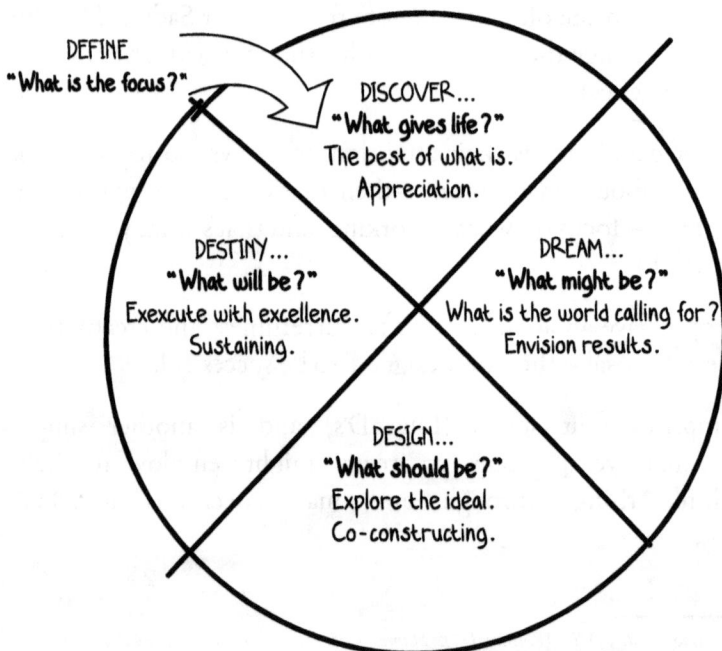

DEFINE
"What is the focus?"

DISCOVER...
"What gives life?"
The best of what is.
Appreciation.

DREAM...
"What might be?"
What is the world calling for?
Envision results.

DESIGN...
"What should be?"
Explore the ideal.
Co-constructing.

DESTINY...
"What will be?"
Exexcute with excellence.
Sustaining.

Some people become concerned when they first encounter AI because they think it is very idealistic and ignores problems. This is not the case. It doesn't ignore the challenges and problems in life – it just approaches them from the other side. Instead of focusing on what is wrong or what is lacking, it chooses to focus on discovering what is working and where, and then creates an environment where people can succeed more. In fact, AI is a supremely practical approach, especially compared with the common approach of focusing only on problems... which of course tends to make the problems grow and dominate our thinking. An appreciative approach generates new energy for the task while a problem-focused approach saps us of energy.

For example, if we relate this to you and your work – a 'standard' performance question is often something like "Where are the gaps in your performance?" That question assumes that you are not already doing what is required. The AI question may be something like this: "When are you most alive and contributing your best?" It assumes that there are already at least some moments when you are currently experiencing success (either at work or elsewhere - even if only now and then) and that you can build upon this. The focus of inquiry is on learning and discovering how the environment – both your internal thinking environment and the external environment you live and work in – might be shaped so that you can contribute your best. It's about discovering how you can set yourself up for success.

Reflections and Fieldwork:

1. Listening deeply requires practice. Plan to focus on this skill in the next few weeks. Really listen to what people are saying. Watch for non-verbal messages too. What is people's reaction to your deep listening?

_____

_____

_____

_____

2. Consider a challenge your team is working with (or should be working with). Try applying the appreciative inquiry process to develop a series of questions you could pose to your team members to help move the challenge forward.

_____

_____

_____

_____

_____

_____

_____

3. In your next team meeting (or similar), try asking some questions that go to the heart of the issue from your perspective. How did people respond to this? What did you observe? What does that mean for you?

_____

_____

_____

_____

_____

_____

_____

4. During the coming two weeks, experiment with an appreciative approach. When you hear people talking, see if you can hear when people are in the 'downward spiral', looking only at the problems or failures, and see if you can change that to 'radiating possibilities' by asking an appreciative question such as: What do we already do well? What successes have we had recently? What is working well now? Jot down some notes after your experiment: What specifically did you do?

_____

_____

_____

   a. What did you see or observe as people reacted to your question?

_____

_____

_____

_____

_____

   b. What difference did it make?

_____

_____

_____

_____

_____

c. What would you do differently if you did it again?

_____

_____

_____

_____

_____

_____

_____

CHAPTER 8

Making your contribution - how do you want the new story to unfold?

Questions addressed in this chapter:

- How can you draw together all the threads that you have revealed to yourself?

- What is your new story?

- What do you need to do now?

We are nearing the end of the book, but perhaps reaching the beginning of new possibilities for you and what the future holds, and how you might take conscious responsibility for shaping or influencing that future.

This last chapter is about how you might become more aware of the future you really want in (or beyond) your workplace and how you might craft a story to remind yourself of that possible future – and perhaps share with others as appropriate.

Stories are important

Stories may seem like kid's stuff, and that is a clue as to why they are so important. Through thousands of years, stories have been used to teach important lessons and maintain important traditions. They are a natural and uncomplicated way to learn – remembering a story is so much easier than remembering facts.

In the book *Treading Lightly: the hidden wisdom of the world's oldest people*, the authors identify how the traditions, landscapes and beliefs of Indigenous Australians were all passed on from one generation to the next through a tightly woven series of stories, dances, songs, paintings, and societal roles.

Stories also manage to convey the complexity of topics and the emotion of the personal perspective – and it seems they can do that without getting caught up in the analytical part of the brain. In this way, new ideas can be conveyed in a manner that resonates directly with the listener. A story seems to 'fly under the radar.' Stories are powerful ways of communicating.

Telling your story

What is the art of telling a good story? Despite what you may think, your own story is as powerful as any! You may think, "No one is interested in my story..." But humans are hardwired to listen to stories. This is how comedians, authors, and film makers all ply their trade. They take the ordinary and weave it into an emotional and powerful story.

You may not consider yourself as someone who is good with words or much of a storyteller, but most of our own 'crises' are what the distinguished American leadership scholar, Warren Bennis, calls crucibles or defining moments in our lives. Bennis describes crucibles as "intense, transformational experiences from which a leader [person] changes dramatically. They are places where essential questions are asked: Who am I? Who could I be? Who should I be? How do I relate to others?"

The key to communicating to others what you have learned in a rich and powerful story is recalling not only what happened to you at that time but also what you were thinking – and feeling. The more you can recall and simply tell what you were thinking and feeling at the time – the more powerful your story will be. Recalling and conveying the emotion you felt is essential.

In thinking about the structure of your story, you might use a simple construct known as the hero's journey. This type of story follows your defining or crucible moment. There is a description of life as it was before the event, followed by details of the event itself and how it affected you and others around you. Then describe what you thought and felt as you grappled with the event and what you learned from it. This flows into the next stage as you describe life after the event.

Telling a story of what might be – your vision

Not all stories are about what has been – some are about what might be. Often these types of stories are called visions. One of the most famous and well-known visions was conveyed by Martin Luther King Jr, in what has become known as his "I have a dream" speech.

The power of these stories lies in the same places as described above. It comes from being able to describe what you want to experience – to see, feel, smell, taste and hear in the future – what is possible, and what it means for you and others. These are stories (like all stories) that are values rich. If you can convey the thinking and the feeling, people will be strongly engaged by your vision.

Not all visions have to be created and shared in this way. Visions can also be co-created by a group and shared because they are co-created. This is more unusual in our traditional organisations, but quite common in not-for-profit or activist settings where the organisation relies upon accessing people's inspiration – their values – rather than payment for services. What would our traditional organisations be like should they be able to tap their workers' inspiration, energy, and discretionary effort through a co-created vision? What mental models prevent us from thinking about and exploring this option?

Your vision of what might be – how you really want to experience work life - is as important as anyone's because you have influence in bringing that vision into reality. You can take conscious responsibility for articulating it and bringing it into being. How can you convey your story and remind yourself of your vision? What if you shared your story with your team leader and/or team?

Reflections and Fieldwork:

1. Recall a time you heard someone tell their own story. What was most powerful about it? What made you interested?

_____

_____

_____

_____

_____

2. Review your notes from our journey together through this book. You might try creating a mind map to capture your learning on one page.

   • What have you become more aware of, and why is that important? (You might consider each of the different topics we have explored.)

   • As you tried out different ideas and new ways of doing things, what worked for you and what didn't? How does that make you feel? What possibilities are opening?

_____

_____

_____

_____

3. Develop your story or vision of how you really want to experience work with your teammates and in service to your team's and organisation's purpose. How do you want to contribute your strengths, values, sense of purpose, past experiences, and skills in service to your team and others? How do you feel about the different elements of that story? Prepare to share your story with your team leader and colleagues. How can they help you bring your vision into being together? How can you help them?

_____

_____

_____

_____

_____

_____

_____

_____

_____

_____

_____

_____

_____

_____

IN CLOSING

This is not the end of the story by any means, but I do hope that the pages in this book have facilitated an interesting part of your path towards more fulfilling, rewarding and joyful work and life.

The major message I would like to leave you with was expressed by Howard Thurman, an American philosopher, theologian, civil rights leader, and author as follows:

"Do not look at the world and ask what needs doing.
Look into yourself and ask what brings you alive -
then go do that.
Because what the world needs is people who have come alive."

Many people are unaware that they can expect to have a life full of those activities that bring the most joy into their lives.

Many people have become caught in the rhythms and patterns of life to the point where they act on automatic pilot – unaware of what is really going on.

Many people are 'victims' of a transaction with 'hero leaders' in positions of authority (and indeed, we suggest those leaders are also victims in this transaction), where the exchange is "I follow you as long as you look after me and if you stuff up, I can blame you – because you are responsible, not me."

Many people are unaware of the unique personal resources they have to contribute to their families, workmates and even our Earth at this time of increasing turmoil and opportunity.

Many people – but not you!

I look forward to seeing the influence of your self-leadership as you make your unique and joyful mark on the world around you – one that sustains you, your team, your organisation, and our Earth.

ABOUT THE AUTHOR

Dr Josie McLean is an experienced and internationally recognised executive coach. Her working background includes roles in corporate strategic planning in the auto and finance industries, merchant banking environment, business finance, business advisor and, since 1999, director of The Partnership.

Personally, Josie is a change agent with a passion for leadership that is not only strongly anchored on personal values and accountability but underpinned by a deep conceptual understanding and acted upon in her own life. Given the context of complex global problems we face, she is committed to assisting people to exercise their leadership for a sustainable global future.

In 2020, Josie published the influential book, *Big Little Shifts: A practitioner's guide to complexity for organisational change and adaptation.*

She is married with three children and enjoys the beach, jazz, reading, and a globally located network of like-minded friends.